This Journal
Belongs to: